LEADERSHIP IS A SUPERPOWER

by Mari Schuh

PEBBLE
a capstone imprint

Published by Pebble, an imprint of Capstone
1710 Roe Crest Drive, North Mankato, Minnesota 56003
capstonepub.com

Library of Congress Cataloging-in-Publication Data is available on the Library of Congress website.
ISBN: 9780756576684 (hardcover)
ISBN: 9780756576639 (paperback)
ISBN: 9780756576646 (ebook PDF)

Summary: You set a good example for your siblings at home. You encourage your friends to make good decisions. At school, you stand up for what's right. These are all ways to show leadership. Find out more ways to show this real-life superpower and why it's so important.

Image Credits
Getty Images: bonniej, 17, Hispanolistic, 13, iStock/Goodboy Picture Company, 16, JGI/Jamie Grill, 15, Marco VDM, 11, Marko Geber, 19, pixdeluxe, 5, Tim Platt, 18, Wanida Prapan, Cover; Shutterstock: Evgeny Atamanenko, 9, Kapitosh, design element (background), Monkey Business Images, 7, ORION PRODUCTION, 20, Prostock-studio, 14, wavebreakmedia, 6

Editorial Credits
Editor: Alison Deering; Designer: Bobbie Nuytten; Media Researcher: Svetlana Zhurkin; Production Specialist: Whitney Schaefer

All internet sites appearing in back matter were available and accurate when this book was sent to press.

Table of Contents

Words in **bold** are in the glossary.

Leadership Matters

Think of a leader you know. Maybe it is your teacher or a coach. Maybe it is your mom or dad. Leaders **encourage** others. They listen. They lead a group toward a **goal**. When people need help, leaders get the job done.

Being a leader isn't always easy. Leaders need to have lots of skills. But being a leader is important. Leaders make a big difference in people's lives.

Leadership is a **superpower**. When you're a good leader, you know how to get along with others. You know how to work together as a team. You make sure to listen. You help your group reach its goals.

Leaders are honest. They treat people fairly. They encourage others. It can be fun to get others excited. Leaders might say, "We can do this!" or "Good job, team!"

Sometimes people forget to be good leaders. They forget to listen. They might be bossy and tell people what to do. When things don't go right, they might make **excuses**. They might **blame** other people.

Good leaders remember to slow down. They are mindful. They admit when they make mistakes. They know it's okay to ask for help.

Being a Leader at Home

Leaders are **responsible**. They lead by example. Sasha takes good care of her dog. She remembers to feed him. She walks him every day. Sasha teaches her brother how to groom their dog. Together, they pick up their dog's toys.

Leaders also think of others. They **volunteer** to help. Pablo helps his mom and dad at dinnertime. They cook the meal together. Pablo helps set the table. He also cleans up after the meal. Pablo sets a good example for his younger sister.

Being a Leader at School

Leaders don't give up. They are creative. They find different ways to solve problems. Leaders are also **confident**. They know they can do it!

Lulu and her classmates are working on a science project. But it is not going well. Lulu asks the group for help. She listens to their ideas and suggestions. The group comes up with new ways to do the project.

Leaders are helpful and **patient**. Jackson is the line leader for his class. He helps the class form one line to go to lunch. Jackson is kind and calm. He leads the way.

Leaders have a positive attitude. Ari is captain of her soccer team. Her team lost the game. Ari encourages her teammates. She tells them that they all played well. Ari also reminds everyone to high-five the other team. They tell the other players they did a great job.

Always Learning

Leaders are not perfect. Sometimes they make mistakes. Leaders know it's okay to admit that. They keep working hard. They are always learning.

Leaders want to keep getting better. They want to work with others to get things done. That's why leadership is a superpower!

Listening Game

Being a good listener is a big part of being a great leader. Good listeners want to learn about others. They ask questions so they can get to know people better. They focus on what other people say. Being a good listener can also help you be a better friend. Try this fun game as a way to practice your listening skills. You will be on your way to being a good leader!

What You Need:

- notebook

- pen or pencil

What You Do:

1. Decide that you are not going to talk about yourself for a whole day. Instead, focus on being a good listener. Write down this goal in your notebook.

2. When you talk to others, ask them questions about themselves. For example: What is your favorite food? Do you have any hobbies? How many siblings do you have?

3. Carry your notebook with you all day. This will remind you of your listening goal.

4. At the end of the day, think about your goal. How did it go? Was it hard to listen? Or was it easy? What did you learn?

5. Write down three things you learned about other people. Or draw a few pictures that show three things you learned about them.

Glossary

blame (BLAYM)—to say that what happened was someone else's fault

confident (KON-fi-duhnt)—sure of oneself

encourage (in-KUHR-ij)—to give praise and support

excuse (ik-SKYOOS)—something offered as a reason for doing something

goal (GOHL)—something that you aim for or work toward

patient (PAY-shunt)—calm during frustrating or hard times

responsible (ri-SPON-suh-buhl)—doing what you say you will do

superpower (SOO-pur-pow-ur)—an important skill that can affect yourself and others in a big way

volunteer (vol-uhn-TIHR)—to offer to do something without pay

Read More

Hancock, James. *Leadership at Home*. Minneapolis: Jump!, 2020.

Hancock, James. *Leadership at School*. Minneapolis: Jump!, 2020.

Rose, Emily. *Taking Responsibility and Being a Leader*. Ann Arbor, MI: Cherry Lake Publishing, 2022.

Internet Sites

PBS Learning Media: Bounce Back with Ruby and Lamar—Resilience and Leadership: TEAMology
https://kcts9.pbslearningmedia.org/resource/resilience-leadership-video/teamology//

PBS Learning Media: Talking About Responsibility: Xavier Riddle and the Secret Museum
https://kcts9.pbslearningmedia.org/resource/responsibility-story/life-lessons-xavier-riddle-and-the-secret-museum/

YouTube: HSBC Kids Explain: Leadership
https://www.youtube.com/watch?v=CsaBZhEzOOU

Index

About the Author

Mari Schuh's love of reading began with cereal boxes at the kitchen table. Today she is the author of hundreds of nonfiction books for beginning readers. Mari lives in the Midwest with her husband and their sassy house rabbit. Learn more about her at marischuh.com.